Rasp

The Essential Guide On Starting Your Own Raspberry Pi 3 Projects With Ingenious Tips & Tricks!

Table of Contents

Introduction

Among many world wonders created by man-kind, technology is the one field whose endless possibilities and applications we have become addicted to. What if I told you, you can think of any application, any application at all and I can derive an algorithm and device a plan to execute it, would you believe me? Raspberry Pi helps you discover that world, filled with possibilities. If you want to tap into the potential that is a Raspberry Pi board, then read further.

There are many boards such as the Raspberry Pi available in the market. The textbook definition of such novices are known as 'Embedded Systems'. Embedded Systems is a field of technology that converts human programmed code into electrical signals that can be understood by a machine. The machine often decodes these signals and executes the instructions written in the program. Adding more adaptable sensors, cameras, software programs, memory devices, etc. you can create a whole new level of applications that can automate just about anything.

Raspberry Pi is essentially created for school and college students who are very much interested in electronics and their application. Numerous kits, projects, accessories and extended appliances are available to help them execute just about any idea that they may have. Once you start to understand how a Raspberry   Pi system works, it awakens a powerful interest in you to explore more. This is the form of interactive, application oriented platform that help in creating not only great engineers but phenomenal inventors.

Even though Raspberry Pi is a small microcontroller unit, we are able to understand the architecture of how a computer and a mobile phone works. This book is aimed at those, irrespective of age, who are just interested in understanding how feasible technology as become and how you can become an inventor too. The more you wonder, the more you learn and derive answers. The more answers you get, the more you create. The more you create and put them together, the better the inventor you become.

In this book, you will first be introduced to Raspberry Pi, its models and their technical terminologies and components. You will get an insight to how you can use these components and what external devices you can add to complement your project. In the computer world, creating is synonymous with coding, so this book will give you an insight on what programming languages you need to learn that is compatible with Raspberry Pi. The most interesting part of it all are the projects. You will get an overview of what types of projects you can do and also a skeletal idea on how to execute it.

Raspberry Pi kits are one of those educational kits used that is very application oriented that it excites students and tests their abilities. It is challenging and yet has the potential to be used in the most creative ways.

I want to thank you for choosing this book and I hope you get a great insight on what Raspberry Pi is and how you can become an innovator.

Chapter 1: Raspberry Pi – An Overview

Have you ever wondered what powers a computer? How does a printer, washing machine, an air conditioner, or simply put, an electronic item work? Any automation of a machine is simply based on an algorithm, that is, the machine gets instructions from the user to execute the various tasks that it is capable of doing.

For example, you need to change the temperature on your air conditioner. The first thing you do is press the relevant buttons either on the remote or the buttons on the machine itself. The air conditioner receives these signals in the form of waves. These waves are detected and decoded as to what the instruction is. Once this is decoded into a machine level language it starts to change the settings in the crevices that are involved in changing the temperature of the air conditioner. All these processes take place in a matter of a second. Receiving signals, decoding and executing instructions are done by the mother board, or something that is referred to as an 'Embedded System'.

When you first look at the Raspberry Pi board, it does resemble a motherboard that you would have seen inside an electronic device. It is a conglomerate of different electrical entities that is crucial in the process of running a computer. This is actually referred to as a 'microcontroller'. Raspberry Pi has many predecessors that have come out with similar ideas and applications, but Raspberry Pi stands out in the market not only because of its highly evolved specifications but also because it features its own operating system. That sounds like a very cheap computer whose specifications you get to design from scratch. Not only do you get to choose the specifications, but you also get to decide what to house your Raspberry Pi in, there are containers are sold for those who would prefer it, while others like the exposed circuit board aesthetic. You have the power to change almost everything about it. Later in the book you will learn about turning your Raspberry Pi into a media center, which serves as a great example of how many different options you truly have. One person chose to hollow out an old amp speaker to keep all the cords and Raspberry inside, because it matched their décor, while another person painted an old apple crate, because it looked best with their rustic decorations. Traditional computers do not give you this amount of freedom.

Raspberry Pi also connects itself to the internet and that gives rise to a plethora of possibilities. Today, the computer professionals and scientists are trying to revolutionize our standard of living by introducing a new concept known as the 'Internet of Things' or IoT. This concept is aimed at connecting all our electronic gadgets in our homes to the internet and can help you control them from a remote location. Let us say, you have left your stove on. The IoT in your house will either automatically switch it off once it senses your absence or notifies of it in your cellphone and you can instruct it to switch it off. Concepts like these can be achieved right now with boards like Raspberry Pi.

Basically, boards like Raspberry Pi will help you execute the kind of automation that you would want in your life, after technology aims at making people's life easier. You can give the Raspberry Pi many different purposes, it can serve as a retro gaming console or even an interactive mirror that feels as though it straight out of the future. It is this freedom that allows you to create the smart house you have always wanted.

Models of Raspberry Pi

Raspberry Pi boards are modelled and developed in the Wales, United Kingdom by the Raspberry Pi foundation. They first came out with Raspberry Pi 1 Model A which is a cheaper model of the Raspberry Pi 1 Model B which was released later in the same year. Raspberry Pi 1 Model B is often referred to as the original model since it included all the features the creators wanted to include in the kit. Model A was like a cheaper preview model whose features could match that of Model B if more peripherals where added. Both models are of the same size and worked on the same processor, whereas Model B is the preferred version since it had more facets that Model A couldn't cover.

Later they came out with Raspberry Pi 1 B+ model, again whose cheaper preview predecessor was Raspberry Pi 1 A+ model. These revisions came out with better memory, faster processing rates and lower costs. These were the preferred models in schools and colleges. Not only did they promote the study of computer science in a school level, but also taught students to be more innovative and interactive. There are multiple forums online where students have taken to creating marvelous projects that can be applicable for day to day use, or in automation in factories and industries, smart technology that can be used by the army, aviation and naval forces and so many more.

The Raspberry Pi 2 Model B used the best from the first models, and made improvements where it could. Much of the software and projects can be used on all models of the Raspberry Pi, which makes it convenient and means that it is not necessary to immediately update if you are not the position to. However, there are some things that will only work on the newest model, so it is wise to take this into consideration when you are working.

The most recent version of these boards is the Raspberry Pi 3 Model B. This is said to have the fastest processor of them all with better memory, user interface and connectivity, graphic interface specifications and many more. We will discuss Raspberry Pi 3 more in detail. However, it doesn't matter which model you have, they are all useful learning tools.

When you begin experimenting and learning to use your Raspberry Pi, you might find that you need extra hardware and different parts. One of the best parts of the Raspberry Pi community is that it is primarily DIY, so many people have taught themselves to use common items to get their desired results. This means that instead of having to spend a bunch of money on new parts, there are cheaper, alternatives such as purchasing used or broken items that can be taken apart and used for your purposes. Not every community is like this, that is just another one of the things that makes the Raspberry Pi so unique, people love to experiment and learn with it, and then pass on their knowledge.

It is also never too late to learn how technology works. Even if it has been years since you were in school, you will still benefit from using the Raspberry Pi. As a matter of fact, when most people begin exploring the possibilities that Raspberry Pi gives them, they want to keep going and create more. It can seem daunting to a complete beginner, because it can feel like a new language, but with anything new, all it takes some patience and practice. So with some determination and patience, you will be well on your way to completing and maybe even inventing a new project.

Chapter 2: Raspberry Pi 3- Model B Hardware Specifications

Raspberry Pi 3 Model B was first released in February 2016 and it surpassed all its predecessors, but remained the same cost as Raspberry Pi 1 model due to the company's effective production optimizations. This helped universities, colleges and schools to invest in more of these boards since they were cost effective and the results so achieved surpasses expectations. Now let us get into the specifications of Raspberry Pi 3.

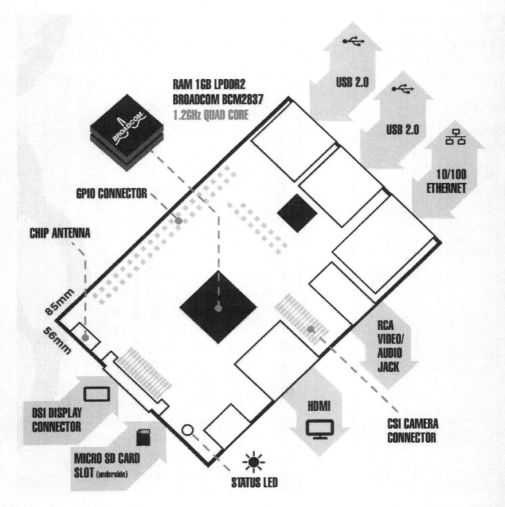

RAM 1GB LPDDR2
BROADCOM BCM2837
1.2GHz QUAD CORE

USB 2.0

USB 2.0

10/100
ETHERNET

GPIO CONNECTOR

CHIP ANTENNA

85mm

56mm

RCA
VIDEO/
AUDIO
JACK

DSI DISPLAY
CONNECTOR

HDMI

CSI CAMERA
CONNECTOR

MICRO SD CARD
SLOT (underside)

STATUS LED

Fig. 1 - Depicts a typical Raspberry Pi 3 - Model B with its hardware components

Hardware

First and foremost, Raspberry Pi is a miniaturized computer, hence it is galvanizations of multiple components that is found in a typical desktop/laptop.

System on Chip – This is the unit of Raspberry Pi 3 that consists of a chip that is used process, like the first generation smart phones, which is manufacture by Broadcom. This is the only model of Raspberry Pi that has the Broadcom BCM2837 SoC (System on Chip) as supposed to BCM2836 in other models.

CPU – The Central Processing Unit of Raspberry Pi 3 consists of an ARM Quad Core processor cortex A53. A general desktop or laptop uses an ARM processor of cortex A15. The older models used ARM1176JZF-S which usually worked in a processing frequency of 700 MHz as supposed to the 1.2GHz produced by the latest version. This chip has dual processing cores that run at 32kB Level ! and 512kB Level 2 cache memory, this is also linked to a 1 GB LPDDR2 memory module that is located on the rear of the board.

GPU – Graphic Processing Unit of all the versions of Raspberry Pi have remained relatively the same, updated as necessary – Broadcom VideoCore IV at 400 MHz with OpenGL ES 2.0 (A graphic interface manufactured especially for Embedded Systems such as Raspberry Pi). It is capable of 25 GFLOPS and is compatible to view MPEG 2 and VC-1. It is also able to render 1080p quality pictures and videos using the H.264/MPEG-4 AVC, a high profile encoder and decoder. The graphics generated using this said have been as good as the ones used in Xbox 360.

Memory – The slot for the MicroSD card to be inserted is available on the flip side of the board and can be used as a detectable memory. These are usually used to store external software, applications, files and documents necessary for the CPU/GPU to use while executing the instructions.

RAM- Random Access Memory has been extended to 1 GB (shared with GPU) that is twice that of its predecessors. This RAM uses about 512 Mb or less with GPU which enables faster rendering of 1080p video decoding or even advanced playing of 3D videos. There other half is used for CPU proceedings. There have been few issues that were reported based on the improper splitting of the RAM.

Ethernet port/USB ports – This jack is used to connect the 8P8C (8 position 8 connector) module that uses a terminally twisted pair cable to connect to the internet physically. This model has a built in Ethernet port that is used to connect into networks. USB ports can be used for similar purposes but it is usually used to add in peripherals like a keyboard or a mouse. Mini-USB jack is used for power.

40 GPIO pins – The 'General Purpose Input Output' pins are a systemically integrated digital control line matrixes which can be configured in a computer algorithm and attach a purpose to it. They are configured by binary signals and which depict input and output. Most of these are connected to peripherals which can be customizable as per the requirements of the project. In addition to these pins there is also pins provided for UART, I2C bus and audio and SPI bus with 2 chip selects.

Audio Ports – The RPi 2 uses the I2C or the Integrated Interchip Sound system that connects various digital audio devices or components together by a serial bus interface standard. It uses higher order PCM encoding and decoding that results in the separation of clock and serial data signals which reduces the 'jitter' and improves audio quality.

CSI (Camera Serial Interface) – Raspberry Pi uses the CSI-2 v1.3 that provides the bandwidth required for the processer to communicate with the peripheral camera that is attached to the RPi 2 board and also exhibits highly flexible channel layout.

DSI (Display Serial Interface) - It is the physical interface that connects the host processor to a peripheral display which may be a projected image display, a Television, computer or even a touch screen. DSI sets specific pixel formats that are required to match the quality specifications of the peripheral defined in MIPI alliance for Display Command Set (DCS) and Display Pixel Interface 2 (DPI-2).

802.11n Wireless LAN – In addition to an Ethernet port, the Raspberry Pi 3 can also connect to the internet wirelessly. This is the first time a model has been able to do this.

Bluetooth 4.1 – Just like with cell phones, the Raspberry Pi 3 will have Bluetooth connectivity, meaning information will be able to be transferred wirelessly, as long as they are within range. This is also the first model to have this function.

Clock – Raspberry Pi is heavily depended on network time server for real time clock and does not possess one on its own.

Power Source – It uses a MicroUSB which provides 5V of electric voltage.

Size – 3.370 in x 2.224 in (same size as the other models except Raspberry Pi Zero)

Cost – Only the Raspberry Pi board typically costs $34.99 US dollars. The peripherals have to be purchases separately.

The newest model is the most convenient because of its ability to connect to the internet wirelessly. For many people, it means that they can work from places other than just their homes, which is very convenient. The Raspberry Pi has always been mobile because of its small size, but with the new model a new layer has been added to its mobility. People can now use their Raspberry Pi's in groups connected to the same network and can even send information via Bluetooth, something that was not possible before. Raspberry Pi users are more connected to each other now than every before with these improvements. Raspberry Pi is just making it easier for the common person to become more in tuned and educated about the way technology works and inspiring a new generation of inventors and engineers.

Chapter 3: Raspberry Pi – Software Specifications

As mentioned before, Raspberry Pi was created for educational purposes rather than industrial ones and hence it encourages students to try and execute programs. The usual preference is generally Python, in fact the Pi from Raspberry Pi comes from the word Python.

Since the technologies are evolving so rapidly it is very hard for us to keep up. Every step of the way you hear new programming languages popping up. In order to overcome this discrepancy Raspberry Pi is compatible with many object oriented programming languages and extends an option of choosing a language that you are most familiar with. This amazing feature has helped these boards reach students across borders who don't necessarily have to learn a new programming language to use these boards.

The use of multiple programming languages will help the product to stay longer in the market and might even become an important tool in learning the electronic science.

Some of the languages that can be used in Raspberry Pi are listed below and keep in mind that this list in not exclusive. More languages can be used and many feature may be added in the future. Any language that can be compiled for ARM Cortex A53 chip can be used to program the Raspberry Pi.

And listed below are the some of the languages used in Raspberry Pi:

Scratch

As an entry level programming language, Scratch has extended the horizons for many computer science enthusiasts. This is a standard in Raspberry Pi distribution known as Raspbian. Lifelong Kindergarten Group in MIT Media Lab, Boston, Massachusetts sowed the idea of Scratch and it was aimed at young students and learner to become more involved in computational and mathematical concepts by hands on experimentation and execution.

Python

This is the standard and primary programming language used on the Raspberry Pi. Python was actually named after the creator's favorite character from the show 'Life of Brian', Monty Python's Flying Circus. There were references of the show citied in the documentation and examples of the language.

Python was one of those languages invented for learner and it was a simple, uncomplicated layout of other languages. This made it a lot easier to execute some iterating statements and made the instructions simple. The projects that are outlined in this book use Python because it so commonly taught and unique to the Raspberry Pi. Even a beginner has the ability to grasp the basics of this language, which is one its major appeals.

HTML5

The World Wide Web is based on a strong foundation of HTML and it was invented by Tim Berners- Lee. It initially started when Lee was working in Geneva and was struggling to find a way to allow organizations to share their documents across offices, towns, cities and even between countries.

It is often referred to as the building block of the internet. It helps the internet to construct the webpages based on the instructions of the web developer and the path it has to follow once a different address is specified. The pages of the web are often interlinked and lead you to pages with different type of content. According to the advancements made in the recent times HTML has also updated itself. The version we are using currently is the HTML5 which has enabled web developer to embed videos or audio in their webpages which was made possible with its radical redesign. HTML5 has also been extended to design apps for mobile phones and tablets.

JavaScript

JavaScript was the secondary addition to HTML that raised the standards of the internet websites through the years. It specifically improved the interactivity and communication between different web users and also connect the systems to a global level. The World Wide Web Consortium were the ones who invented and maintained this scripting language besides HTML and CSS.

JavaScript added a new niche of sophistication to the websites and also allowed customization so that the web developers become more and more innovative as the time passed. New options such as the roll over buttons, drop down menus, advertisement marquees, calculations etc. were possible using JavaScript. Later on, JavaScript combined with XML to become AJAX, scripting languages now adopted by companies such as Google and Yahoo! The usability of online maps, news, and even web searches became far easier with this programming language.

JQuery

JQuery is said to be a simpler and less complicated version of HTML whose syntax and semantics are far easier to comprehend and execute. JQuery also added a lot of interactive components and enabled developers to create rich web interfaces with just a small amount of JavaScript knowledge.

Java

Java is one of the most celebrated programming languages that was compatible across platforms and operating systems alike. This programming language was the boom of the Silicon Valley due it its simplistic nature and its ability to be used in any system whether it was Windows or Unix boxes, without having to reprogram the code according to their standards.

This language brought about a universality among computer that surged up a huge wave of computer engineers and scientists to rely on this language for their programming needs. This language also dominated the Information Technology scene for a couple of years. A few lines of code could run across different platforms, can be successfully executed in a Raspberry Pi board.

C programming language

The C programming languages predominated the Embedded Systems scene even before the computer was popularized. C language was one of the predominating languages using which Linux was written and since it is the operating system on the Raspberry Pi, it is one of the ideal languages you can use on it.

C programming gave rise to the widely used programming languages we used today such as Python, Java, JavaScript and a successor of this language called D. The extension of this language called the Objective C is used as a predominant script to write apps on the iPhones and iPads.

C++

C++ was the first of its kind to be an object oriented based programming, that is, it based its output on real time objects and computation. It was created by a Danish developer Bjarne Stroustrup as an attempt to enhance C. It is used in smorgasbord of applications, including as an embedded software, hardware design, programming video games, graphical applications and as an extension even to set up a website. C++ added what was lacking in C, the object oriented output and became a base for the programming languages used today such as Java, Smalltalk, Ruby and .Net.

Perl

Perl plays an important role of cohesively binding the internet together and is often referred to as 'Swiss Army Chainsaw of scripting languages'. Before Perl, the internet was a collection of static webpages linked together, Perl brought in a versatile flexibility and adaptability that websites could be put together on the fly. Internet soon became a dynamic and adaptable environment that suited the user's needs. These brought about the adaptability of the user's web content based on his or her previous searches or the location he or she is living in. This extended hands and enabled ecommerce such as Amazon and eBay. This by extension helps the Raspberry Pi interfaces to connect to the internet.

Erlang

Erlang is one of the most foolproof programming languages which give a very low margin for mistakes or error to take place while executing. Matters of high order precedence such as planning an air traffic control system, bank/home security system, running a nuclear power plant etc. are highly dependent on Erlang since its high reliability prevents system failure and any type of accidents from happening.

Erlang is usually implemented on systems which have heavy back up and can immediately recruit the stand-by system in case the working one fails. As talked about before Raspberry Pi can also be used to make applications for the Military, Navy and Air Forces, where programming languages like Erlang come into play.

You can choose which language you are most comfortable with or what works best with the specific project you are working on. Keep in mind, for the beginner, this can be overwhelming, but all it takes is some practice. So, try not to get frustrated in the beginning, it is not uncommon to stumble through it at first. Simply choose an easier project at first, because even the simplest of projects will still teach you so much. Once you have completed your first project, the sense of accomplishment will often lead to a desire to learn and do more, making learning fun and give you something functional in the end.

Chapter 4: How to Install a Software on Raspberry Pi

Raspberry Pi has a great standing in the market as one of the best learning platforms, today because when compared to the other boards in market, Raspberry Pi stands out when it comes to its flexibility and compatibility of its operating system. In order to implement computing projects or gaming, from media centers and NAS boxes to Android emulation, you need to learn to install software to run on the computer.

This installation could mean anything from installing an operating system to installing an application from the Raspberry Pi store or other repositories. These are just as easy as installing an app in your computer or your phone. If you are new to Linux then it may a little unfamiliar to you but it is nothing you can't learn if you just observed. But be warned, the installation of an operating system on to the Raspberry Pi board is rather unusual.

First and foremost you need to be comfortable enough to know your way around a system for you to successfully install an operating network. You will need your desktop or your laptop with Windows, Mac or Linux computer for you to install an operating system. The Raspberry Pi, as you know is flexible mini-computer which can operate on Operating System of your choice. You need to load it onto the MicroSD Memory card that can be used to erase and reinstall at any point in time.

Once the operating system has been successfully loaded on to the SD card, it should be carefully inserted back into the Raspberry Pi on the slot available on the flip side of the board. Boot up the system and the installation will begin shortly after the system is unzipped and systematically organized into their respective directories. Once this is over the Operating System of your choice will start to boot. Operating Systems such as the Debian based Raspbian and the XBMC built

Raspbmc are designed exclusively for The Raspberry Pi devices and it based on Linux OS.

After the operating system is done installing, the device is ready to install software in it. One way to start the installation is by giving out a command line.

For example, you can install the Scrot tool and give a specific command to install software and it goes as:

Sudo apt-get install scrot

The syntax apt-get install is in charge of searching for all the available repositories that the software may require, identifies and downloads the required files. There may be other prompts and interactions that you will face before the operating system is installed. Additional folders and files maybe downloaded which are related but non-essential for the software to run. Do download these files as they give you a better user experience.

Raspberry Pi Store

Linux has always been a unique product in the market and stands out distinctly from the others, and so the executives have tried different ways of making it more user friendly and released Linux versions such as Ubuntu and Mint. These versions make it easier to install software on to the Raspberry Pi board.

First, the package manager acts like a search engine to filter and select the application or software that you want to install. These software repositories are available in a particular distro, similar to a command line with a mouse driven user interface.

Second place to find software are the software centers or those which are infamously known as 'app stores'. Raspberry Pi has its own store where you can download software from known as the 'Raspberry Pi store'.

You need to start a command line for you to successfully install a software from either of these places. The command is:

Sudo apt-get update && sudo apt-get install pistore

Just like a computer installation of a software, a new icon will appear on the desktop after the installation is over. To open, double click on the icon and it opens a window filled with the available applications that you can download. Like the Apple App store or the Google Play store, Raspberry Pi store contains the list of apps, with technical information and screenshots of the app.

Much similar to the installation of an application on a phone or a computer, installation of an App from the Raspberry Pi store is straightforward. Sign in or create an account in the Raspberry Pi store. Start searching for the apps that you would like to download and click on the install button if you would like to purchase it. There are multiple payment methods available for this store and chose the one you would normally use. Once the payment is over the installation starts. Since Raspberry Pi is a miniaturized version of a computer with lesser RAM, you cannot install multiple applications at the same time.

The Raspberry Pi store offers many useful apps created for Pi such as LibreOffice, FreeCiv and OpenTTD. Many more revisions are said to arrive at the store with Raspberry Pi's gaining popularity.

With the software and applications installed on the Raspberry Pi board, it becomes like a compact computer or a cellphone that you can carry around. This computer can be incorporated in so many fascinating projects.

The most challenging thing about installing the software is learning the right commands and where to give them in order to install them. Even though it is a challenge, the board was created for teaching purposes on how to code. This becomes a creative way to get kids and elders alike, interested in the board.

If you want to keep up with what other amateur users and coders have been creating, you can log on to various websites and forums. You can also install the Raspberry Pi store on your computer and check for application updates.

In general, most of the user generated software and apps other users have created is free or very cheap. One user is known for turning his Raspberry Pi into a fully functional smart phone, he created the software that needs to be installed himself and made it available to students and others users as a free download. In case you were considering trying this, it is one of the more advanced projects because of all of the different aspects, but turning your Raspberry Pi into a "smartish" phone is one of the easier beginner projects.

Chapter 5: Configuring Raspberry Pi after Installation

Installing an operating system and adding other software and applications is just the tip of an iceberg, because the possibilities seem to be endless. When first introduced to the Raspberry Pi, they immediately start using it as a media center or a phone if you will. Switching it on, playing around with the applications, doesn't even tap into the potential of what you can do with this pocket sized computer.

The best way to do that is to first configure your Raspberry Pi. The most popular OS used on the Pi is the Debian distro for Linux on a Raspbian platform. Though it is said to run even a windows 8, you have to consider the processor limits on the board. Windows 8 requires a lot more power than what the board can offer and it will ultimately slow your processing speed and even simple applications like searching the web or checking email will be slower than what we are used to now. There are various configurations for the Raspberry Pi that are explained below.

Since the Raspbian OS is unfamiliar to a lot of us, let us take a minute to explore the configuration menu. The configuration menu should automatically pop up when you are trying to install the software, but in case you've missed the step then enter this command to take a closer look at the configuration options:

Sudo raspi-config

Wait until the menu items are loaded on the screen. Using the arrows on your keyboard try to navigate through options until you reach the option you want to select. Then press the enter key on your keyboard.

Following is a list of menu options and what you can find in them:

Info: It contains basic information about the model and settings already set by the factory. It throws a warning message if you are customizing the Raspberry Pi installation too much.

Expand_rootfs- If your SD card is over 4GB, it will dedicate the entire card to the Operating System rather than splitting it.

Overscan- This enables us to remove the black border that hinders us from using the entire display for output. If there is an error, you can rectify it by using edit/boot/config.txt to undo.

Configure_keyboard- This is used to specify the type of keyboard you are using and the language on the keyboard. The default language for Raspberry Pi is UK English.

Change_pass – This option allows you to create your own username and password. The default username is 'pi' and its password is 'raspberry'. Ou can configure them easily by following the instructions you see on the screen.

Change_locale- This menu is very detailed and a little slow to open. The default setting here is en_GU UTF-8, that is, the UTF-8(a character encoding and decoding process which has the ability to convert the information into Unicode) character set available is for English. If you want to add more languages or change the default language, press the spacebar to toggle selections in the menu.

Change_Timezone - Raspberry Pi does not have a default real time clock embedded on the board. Your board is reliant on the operating system for time. You need to first enter your continent, your country and then your city to select your time zone.

Memory_split- This option explicitly allows you to determine the memory that has be allocated for the standard processes and the video core. The main three choices used in Raspberry Pi is 32 Mb, 64 Mb or 128 Mb for processing the video core. Many users have confirmed to the fact that this dock lets them view 1080p quality pictures or slow 3D videos. However, the GPU doesn't have the capability to process them both at the same time. The default option and the highest option for running XBMC on your Raspberry Pi is 64 Mb.

Overclock – Though it is an option that is used in very few applications, many users have advised the beginners to not change any default settings until you someone experienced is helping you.

Ssh- This option is enabled by default and is employed in providing command line access to your Raspberry Pi board from another remote computer. A SSH client such as Putty, is used in executing this command. You can disable this if you are directly connected to the internet through an Ethernet port.

Boot_behavior- You can toggle around with the options on how you want your Raspberry Pi to display after booting either the desktop or a command line.

Update- With new innovations and upgrades around every corner, you need to keep your Raspberry Pi up to date. This option gives you the details and helps you upgrade it. Depending on what you are using your Raspberry for, updating more often might be necessary. This is important because it will get rid of any bugs or kinks and allow your system to run as smoothly as possible.

Using any of these options to change settings will trigger a force reboot which sometimes boots on the command line. If you face such a problem, launch the mouse-driven GUI (Graphic User Interface) by typing the startx command. However, be patient because sometimes Raspberry Pi will need to reboot a couple of times, depending on the software. So, before you get frustrated and give up, make sure you research whether or not it will take only one or more reboots. Another thing to consider is that installation can take a while and the Raspberry Pi might not be as fast as what most people are accustomed to on their laptops, so be patient and wait it out.

Securing your Raspberry Pi

Even though configuring the Raspberry Pi is important, you need to secure your Pi from external threats. Changing the default password can be easily be done by changing the password using raspi_config (by following the instructions written above) or by using the standard Linux passwd command.

You need to ensure that all installations regarding the security updates have been done properly. If you are skipping this step then you have to have to very carefully while connecting to the internet. It is recommended that you don't connect to the internet with securing your Raspberry Pi. There is a simple solution to this problem that can be eradicated using raspi_config menu.

Open the window and type the following:

Sudo apt-get update

Sudo apt-get upgrade

Remember that this is a mini computer which has a low processing power compared to your phones and laptops. It will take a while for it to finish installing, so be patient!

Even though Raspberry Pi is one of the cheapest learning tools out there, its main advantage lies on the fact that it is an open source technology with accessibility to all its key components. Its versatility is its key factor for becoming so popular in the electronics world. Its rudimentary make up has not deterred it from being one of the most innovative tools that can used to create many, many applications. This device is far more powerful and multi-compartmental than a typical computer or a microcontroller.

Chapter 6: Guidelines to Execute Your Own Raspberry Pi Project

So far this book has been raving about how you can create your own project and that the possibilities are endless. We have even covered the guide on how to install an operating system and how to configure the Raspberry Pi. Now it is time for you to get your creative juices following, because creating projects is the fun part.

If you look again at the specifications of the Raspberry Pi 3 Model B, you will come to know that it has bare minimum components. For you to execute any type of project you need to determine what are the peripherals you will need? Where and how do you get them?

Most Raspberry Pi models and its peripherals are available at:

- Adafruit
- Amazon
- Allied Electronics (Only for those living in North America)

The costs are listed below:

- Raspberry Pi 3 Model B - $35
- Raspberry Pi 3 Starter kit - $80
- Universal Power Supply - $5
- Raspberry Pi case - $6
- Raspberry Wi-Fi Dongle - $5
- NOOBS 8 Gb memory card - $4
- Raspberry Pi 7 inch Display - $60
- Raspberry Pi camera and mount - $27.90
- Raspberry Pi Infrared camera and mount - $27.90
- Broadcom USB hub and Wi-Fi adapter - $11.16

Please refer to the official peripheral list provided in the website before purchasing or else it might not be compatible with the Raspberry Pi you have. Also check if any of the peripherals you have lying in your house are compatible with your board. You may not need to spend extra money on those.

The Questions you need to ask before starting a project:

- When you start with a project, be very clear on what you want your outcome to be. Be very clear about the end result so that you can build your project from there.
- What can the Raspberry Pi board do for you to achieve this result?
- Is it going to compile a list of sensory results?
- Is it supposed to send the result to you or proceed to the next course of action on its own?
- If you want a notification, how do you plan on getting it?
- What sort of a signal is your output?
- What are the peripherals you might need to get this output?
- What are the programming languages you can use in order to execute this result?

Once you have answers to these questions, you can proceed to do your project.

Here is a sample project that many Raspberry Pi users have tried. It is a 'Home Automation' using Raspberry Pi. The objective of this project is to detect or sense any motion of a person or an animal on my doorstep and notify it to me. This project can evolve in so many directions but for now let us look at the project guidelines.

What can the Raspberry Pi board do for you to achieve this result?

The Raspberry Board has sense the motion around my doorstep and notify it to me on my cellphone.

Is it going to compile a list of sensory results?

Yes the Raspberry Pi needs to collect information about the motion senses. This can be executed by using PIR sensors. PIR (Passive

Infrared) sensors are usually hooked up with a light. When there is an obstruction of light, the PIR sensors use its signals to detect motion and can send information about it to you on your phone.

Is it supposed to send the result to you or proceed to the next course of action on its own?

It is supposed to send a notification to me through my mobile phone.

If you want a notification, how do you plan on getting it?

The Raspberry Pi board should be connected to a GSM (Global System for Mobile Communications) module that will send me a message.

What sort of a signal is your output?

A message in my mobile.

What are the peripherals you might need to get this output?

A relay network board – this is used to power up your Raspberry Pi board and the external circuitry.

A PIR sensor – It is used for motion detection.

Light sensor – This provides the light required for the PIR sensor to detect motion.

A MicroSD card – this card should contain a preinstalled Operating system and Raspbian Home+

Internet connection – Wireless or through an Ethernet connection, just make sure it is a solid, fast connection.

What are the programming languages you can use in order to execute this result?

This has a preinstalled software called home+ which allows you to configure the GPIOs without the help of a programming language.

Step by Step guideline on how you can execute this project:

1. Take out your Raspberry Pi board and all the peripherals you have listed in order to execute the project.
2. Plan and systematically assign the GPIO pins each peripheral. Remember, each sensor will come with its own power and earth pin.
3. Keeping the order of your GPIO pins, use the 40 pin matrix to set up you peripherals one by one.
4. Add your relay peripheral, 2 pins allocated for power (5 V) and ground and 4 pins allocated for input/outputs from the Raspberry Pi board to the system.
5. Next comes the PIR sensor, 2 pins for power (5 V) and ground and 1 for sensory output from the sensor
6. Connect your light sensor next, 2 pins for power (3 V) and 1 pin for the sensory output from the sensor.
7. Connect the GSM module, 2 pins for power (5 V) and 1 pin for output.
8. Now check if the pins are in the exact places as per your plan
9. Once the pins are in place, it is time to insert the MicroSD memory card containing a preinstalled Operating system and the Home+ software.
10. Connect the Raspberry Pi board to the Ethernet using a twisted pair cable or an optical fiber cable.
11. Now connect the Raspberry Pi board to the power supply through the micro USB port which is allocated specifically for power supply.
12. Boot the board and connect it to a computer. Once you connect it to the computer open the software R PI Home+ or open a web browser and find the IP address of your Raspberry Pi module.
13. Once you have entered your username and password, you will be able to configure the pins and settings of your Raspberry Pi board.

14. Click on the settings and find out the settings for GPIO pins and click on Edit.
15. This will lead to a page where all the 40 pins are listed.
16. Choose the pin you have selected for light sensor and change the output to 'Digital Input', in the next drop down select 'show in homepage' and rename it as Light sensor. Save the changes you have done.
17. Repeat the steps for the PIR sensor, the GSM Module (Except here select 'output state' instead of 'digital input') and the three outputs from the relay network (Except here select 'output state' instead of 'digital input').
18. Once you have saved the changes, it will take you to the home page where the list of inputs and outputs are displayed.
19. Go to the I/O selection page and configure your input. Add turn on task for light sensors so that they are switched on for the PIR sensors to detect motion
20. Repeat the steps for the other inputs and outputs.

Now it is time for you to experiment and see if your project works.

With an object in your hand, move it around the light sensors first. See of the LED blinks on the board and is detected in your home page. Similarly repeat the steps to see if the PIR sensor is working. Once the LEDs are blinking from your movements then the Raspberry Pi has detected motion and triggers the GSM module (Further configuration of the GSM module and your cellphone has to be done before you receive a message in your phone.)

This is sample project that you can execute by simply purchasing a Raspberry Pi Model and learning to configure it.

Now that you have learnt how to execute a real time project that can used to automate your home security, it can be extended in so many ways. You could include a camera peripheral and program the Raspberry Pi board to send you a photo or a video surveillance of the person standing on your doorstep. By connecting your phone and your locks, you can automatically let the person inside your building, this can again be done by PHP networks. You can find a way to connect every electronic item such as the fans, lights, thermostat, screens, ovens, heaters, garage doors etc. to an app in your phone using Raspberry Pi. Like I told you the possibilities are endless!

This is just an example, but many projects are going to need the same things such as a power source and an internet connection. That being said, once you have successfully completed some projects it will be second nature to just include these items in your list. The projects that are explained in the next chapter will include which type of power sources to include, whether it be a USB pack that plugs into the wall or a battery pack for mobility. Again, also remember that used parts and second hand stores can be a wealth of cheap, but perfectly suitable parts for you. This is good for people who worry about the cost of the parts they need.

Try and read about the different modules and peripherals that is available in the market. Even though Raspberry Pi is aimed at students to learn computer science, many of them have taken it as a challenge to create complex applications and projects.

Chapter 7: Programming in Raspberry Pi

Like the software list that is mentioned above, you can use a programming language of your choice on a Raspberry Pi module. Raspberry Pi primarily uses Python for coding its algorithm as it is the most compatible with the Linux Operating system.

Python was initially created to use as a teaching language and hence its instruction and syntax were straightforward and uncomplicated. This language was also used across operating systems and seemed to reduce the number of instructions, when compared to other programmable languages and produce the same output. It soon saw a surge in popularity in the world of embedded systems and other applications due to its simple structure.

For you to start programming a Raspberry Pi board, you need to understand basic concepts in python programming such as variables, constants, loops, basic operators, decision making, lists, functions, modules etc. Here is a quick overview of these concepts.

Python is a general purpose programming language that is object oriented and is a high level programming language.

Overview of Python Programming:

- Python is simple to understand: Python programs usually use syntaxes that are easy to comprehend and it is compiled during the runtime. You will be notified of the mistake you may have made in the syntax before execution.
- Python is interactive: Python can be used as a language to develop situations in which questions can be asked and the answers are processed and prompted in the output.
- Python is a beginner's language: It is a great language to learn if you are just starting out in learning computing languages. It supports a large range of applications across the World Wide Web to a simple text processing.

- Python is object oriented: Like C++, Python aims are Object oriented programming where the output is a real time application. Many of its concepts are borrowed by Python.

Python is accessible across almost all operating systems and machines. Here is the list of operating systems in which it can be installed in:

- Windows CE
- Win 9x/NT/2000
- OS/2
- DOS (multiple versions)
- VMS/OpenVMS
- Psion
- VxWorks
- PalmOS
- UNIX (Solaris, Linux, FreeBSD, AIX, HP/UX, SunOS, IRIX, etc.)
- Acorn/RISC OS
- BeOS
- Macintosh (Intel, PPC, 68K)
- Amiga
- QNX
- Nokia mobile phones
- Python has also been ported to the Java and .NET virtual machines
- Basic Syntax

There are primarily two types of programming:

Interactive Mode Programming: Trying to invoke the interpreter by passing a command to read and respond to the instructions in the code is known as Interactive Mode Programming.

If you type the following:

Print ('Hello, Python!');

It will prompt an output like this:

>> Hello, Python!

Script Mode Programming: Trying to invoke the interpreter with a script parameter which in turn begins to execute the entire length of the script until it reaches the end of the program. This is known as Script Mode Programming.

Assuming that the interpreter has the path to the script containing the file to be executed and is visible we can prompt this:

$ python test.py

And the output will be:

Hello, Python!

Python identifiers: These are a user defined words that can be used as a variable, constant, module, class or a function. An identifier can contain A to Z, a to z, numbers (0 to 9) and underscores. Any other special character will throw an error.

Reserved words: There are a list of keywords that are reserved for specific tasks and functions and they cannot be used as an identifier. For example, the word 'print' cannot be an identifier since that word already serves another purpose. All python keywords should contain small letters only.

Here is the list of reserved words:

And	exec	Not
Assert	finally	Or
Break	for	Pass

Class	from	Print
Continue	global	Raise
Def	if	Return
Del	import	Try
Elif	in	while
Else	is	with
Except	lambda	yield

Basic Operators in Python

These operators perform basic mathematical and logical operations based on the user given input and generate an output for the logic.

Here is the list of operators:

- Arithmetic Operators
- Logical Operators
- Assignment Operators
- Identity Operators
- Comparison (Relational) Operators
- Membership Operators
- Bitwise Operators

Arithmetic Operators:

These operators perform basic arithmetic operations such as addition ('+'), subtraction ('-'), multiplication ('*'), division ('/'), modulus ('%')

which gives the remainder after division of two terms, exponent ("**")
etc. They are used in places where mathematical calculations need to
be done.

Logical Operators:

They perform simple logical tasks such as AND (where both
condition A and condition B are true), OR (where either condition A
or condition B is true) and NOT (where the output is the opposite of
input).

Assignment Operators:

They are the operators that is used to make logical or arithmetic
equations. '=' is used to assign value to the variables, '+=' is used to
added the right operand and assign the value to the left operand, '-=',
'*=', '/=' are also used same as the addition add operator and the
value is assigned to the left operand.

Identity Operators:

They are operators that identify the credibility of a statement by
assigning 'is' for the statements where the operands on either side of
the equation point towards the same object then shows 'true', if not it
shows 'false'. 'Is not' is an operator that checks if the operands on
either side of equation don't point to the same object then it is 'true',
or else it is 'false'.

Comparison Operators:

These are the operators that help in comparing two quantities and
compute an output based on that observation. '==' is equal to, '!=' is
not equal to, '>' is the greater than symbol, '<' is the less than symbol,
'>=' is the greater than or equal to symbol and '<=' is the less than or
equal to symbol.

Bitwise Operators:

These operators perform various tasks for the numbers in their binary form. For instance let us take

A: 0 0 0 1 1 1 1 0

B: 1 1 0 0 0 0 1 1

_____

A&B: 0 0 0 0 0 0 1 0

A|B: 1 1 0 1 1 1 1 1

A^B: 1 1 0 1 1 1 0 1

~A: 1 1 1 0 0 0 0 1

Membership Operators:

These operators test for membership in sequence such as lists, strings, tuplets etc. They are 'in' which checks a sequence and evaluates as 'true' if found in a sequence or 'false' otherwise. 'Not in' checks a sequence for the specified character and if it is missing it reports 'true' or reports 'false' if found in the sequence.

Sample program:

The program written below is a Raspberry Pi specific Python code that has programmed the GPIO pins available on the board and has assigned to a function.

#blink.py //opens the file containing the instructions

Import RPi.GPIO as GPIO //sets the default instructions to include GPIO port

Import time //Used to keep time

GPIO.setmode(GPIO.BOARD)

GPIO.setup(7, GPIO.OUT)

While true:

GPIO.output(7, True)

Time.sleep(0.2)

GPIO.output(7, False)

Time.sleep (0.2)

This is a python program written to execute the blinking of the LED. In the main program, the GPIO pin 7 is initialized. A while loop has started and once the logic in 'blink.py' is true, the loop with iterate until it is false. Inside the loop, if the GPIO 7 logic is true, the LED is switched ON for 0.2 seconds and if the GPIO 7 logic is false it switches OFF for 0.2 seconds. The loop will execute this indefinitely until the Raspberry Pi is switched off because there is no false condition for the while loop to stop.

Common Python Errors and How to Fix Them

The way Python is set up is supposed to be very user friendly, but can still be very difficult for first time users. It might take a while to become fluent in the ways of the program. Here are some common issues and how to fix them:

Confusing expressions and defaults for function based arguments – Python gives you the chance to identify that a function argument is an option by offering a default value for it. This is a wonderful feature of Python's language, but it can still cause confusion when the default value remains mutable. Here is a an example of a Python function definition:

>>> def foo(bar=[ ]) :   # bar is an option and defaults to [ ] if not specified

... bar.append ("baz")   # this line could be a problem, as you can see

... return bar

The error here, is that it is not wise to think that the optional argument will be automatically made to match default expression every time the function is used without providing a value for optional argument. In the code above, for instance, it is easy to expect that calling foo ( ) would continuously return ' baz ' because it would be assumed that a every time foo ( ) is used bar is set to [ ]. This is what happens when you actually do this:

>>> foo ( )

["baz"]

>>> foo ( )

["baz" , "baz"]

>>> foo ( )

["baz" , "baz" , "baz"]

It kept changing the default value of "baz" to an existing list every time foo ( ) was used, instead of making a new list. In advanced Python programming the default value associated with a function argument is calculated only one time, and it is at that one time that the function is defined. This means that the bar argument is initialized to its own default, but only if foo ( ) is first defined, this means that anymore calls to foo ( ) will be used in the same list to which bar was initially initialized.

This is how to fix the issue:

>>> def foo (bar=None) :

. . . if bar is None;

. . . bar = [ ]

. . . bar.append("baz")

. . . return bar

. . .

```
>>> foo ( )
[ "baz" ]
>>> foo ( )
[ "baz" ]
>>> foo ( )
[ "baz" ]
```

Not using class variables properly –

```
>>> class A(object) :
. . . x = 1
. . .
>>> class B(A) :
. . . pass
. . .
>>> class C(A) :
. . . pass
. . .
>>> print A.x, B.x, C.x
1 1 1
```

This one makes sense, as a starting off point, but let's continue:

```
>>> B.x = 2
>>>print A.x, B.x, C.x
1 2 1
```

This also makes sense and is right.

>>> A.x = 3

>>> print A.x, B.x, C.x

3 2 3

Hold on, only A.x was supposed to be changed, so why did C.x change as well? In Python, variables are handled internally as dictionaries and abide by what is usually called the Method Resolution Order or MRO. In the code above the x attribute is not found in class C, instead it will be looked up by base classes, which in the example is only A. Basically, this just means that C does not have its own x property that is separate from A. So when C.x is referenced, it is actually sent to A.x.

Make sure to use correct parameters – This is an example of code:

>>> try :

...   1 = ["a" , "b" }

...   int (1[2])

...   except ValueError, IndexError: # To catch both exceptions, right

...   pass

...

Traceback   (most recent call last) :

File "<stdin>" , line 3, in <module>

IndexError : list index out of range

The issue in this code is that the except statement actually does not include a list of exceptions that are properly specified. When it says except Exception, e is meant to connect the exception to what you have made the optional second specified parameter, in the example, it would be e, this makes it available for more inspection if necessary. This results in an IndexError exception that is not being properly used by the except statement, but instead it winds up being bound to a parameter called IndexError.

The correct way to use multiple exceptions within an except statement is to specify a parameter as a tuple which contains all of the exceptions that will be caught. In addition, it is also a good idea, for portability to use the as keyword, because that kind of syntax is more universal.

```
>>> try:
...     1 = ["a , "b"]
...     int (1[2])
...     except (ValueError, IndexError) as e:
...     pass
...
>>>
```

Mistaking Python scope rules – When it comes to Python scope, it is based on the Local, Enclosing, Global, Built-In rule. This might seem pretty straight forward, but there are actually many aspects of this that can cause errors in Python. Here is an example of common code that might cause you a problem:

```
>>> x = 10
>>> def foo():
...     x += 1
...     print x
...
```

```
>>> foo()
```

Traceback (most recent call last):

  File "<stdin>", line 1, in <module>

  File "<stdin>", line 2, in foo

UnboundLocalError: local variable 'x' referenced before assignment

The problem occurs because when an assignment to a variable in a scope is made, Python automatically assumes it to be local to that scope, this will cause it to shadow any equally named variable. It can surprise you, when you get the UnboundLocalError in code that worked just minutes before just by adding the assignment statement in the function body. It is also common when using lists as well:

```
>>> lst = [1, 2, 3]
>>> def foo1():
...     lst.append(5)   # This works ok...
...
>>> foo1()
>>> lst
[1, 2, 3, 5]


>>> lst = [1, 2, 3]
>>> def foo2():
...     lst += [5]     # ... but this bombs!
...
>>> foo2()
```

Traceback (most recent call last):

File "<stdin>", line 1, in <module>

File "<stdin>", line 2, in foo

UnboundLocalError: local variable 'lst' referenced before assignment

This code would cause foo1 to run properly, but foo2 to mess up. The reason this happened in this previous coding example is the same as in the first, and in this case, foo1 does not connect to an assignment to 1st, but foo2 is. It is important to note, 1st += [5] really just means lst = lst + [5], this is an attempt to assign a value to 1st, but the value given to it is based on 1st itself, which Python assumes is local scope, but it has not really been defined.

Changing a list and iterating over it – Take issue in the following should be obvious:

```
>>> odd = lambda x : bool(x % 2)

>>> numbers = [n for n in range(10)]

>>> for i in range(len(numbers)):

...     if odd(numbers[i]):

...             del numbers[i]   # BAD: Deleting item from a list while iterating over it

...
```

Traceback (most recent call last):

        File "<stdin>", line 2, in <module>

IndexError: list index out of range

Any experienced software developer knows that deleting an item from an array or list while iterating over it will cause a problem. The coding above contains a more blatant mistake, but not all of these will be this easy to see, and it can still trip up even advanced developers.

Python uses many different programming paradigms that simplify and streamline code. An added benefit of simpler code is that it generally creates less opportunity for mistakes. One of the paradigms is the list comprehension paradigm, which is very useful for avoiding this very issue. Here is an example of an alternative code that works properly:

```
>>> odd = lambda x : bool(x % 2)
>>> numbers = [n for n in range(10)]
>>> numbers[:] = [n for n in numbers if not odd(n)]  # ahh, the beauty of it all
>>> numbers
[0, 2, 4, 6, 8]
```

Not fully understanding how Python binds closures – Look at the following code:

```
>>> def create_multipliers():
...     return [lambda x : i * x for i in range(5)]
>>> for multiplier in create_multipliers():
...     print multiplier(2)
...
```

You would anticipate the following ouput:

```
0
2
4
6
8
```

This is actually very different from what you would actually get with that code:

8

8

8

8

8

This occurs because of the late binding behavior of Python, the values of variables used in closures are looked up when the inner function is called. In the code each time the returned functions are called, the value of i is found in the surrounding scope when it is called. Some people think that the solution to this is more of a hack, but there is a solution:

```
>>> def create_multipliers():
...     return [lambda x, i=i : i * x for i in range(5)]
...
>>> for multiplier in create_multipliers():
...     print multiplier(2)
...
0
2
4
6
8
```

The solution is using the default arguments that create anonymous functions in your favor, to achieve your preferred results. Some people do not agree with this type of solution, but it can be helpful to understand how it works anyway.

Circular module dependencies - Assume that you have two files, a.py and b.py and both of them imports the other:

In a.py :

```
import b
def f():
    return b.x
print f()
```

In b.py:

```
import a
x = 1
def g():
    print a.f()
```

First attempt to import a.py:

```
>>> import a
1
```

As it turns out, that works perfectly, there is a properly made circular import. These types of imports are not a problem because Python knows not to try to import the same thing twice, but it does depend on the point at which the module is attempting to access variables or functions defined as the other that problems can arise. When you look at the example provided, a.py did not have a problem importing b.py because it does not need anything from a.py to be defined at the time of import. However, the only reference to b.py to a is a.f(), but the call is g(), but there is no reason for either a.py or b.py to invoke g().

Here's what would happen if you tried to import b.py:

```
>>> import b
```

Traceback (most recent call last):

```
File "<stdin>", line 1, in <module>
    File "b.py", line 1, in <module>
import a
    File "a.py", line 6, in <module>
  print f()
    File "a.py", line 4, in f
  return b.x
AttributeError: 'module' object has no attribute 'x'
```

This wouldn't work because while importing b.py Python also tries to import a.py, thus calling f() which then tries to accss b.x., which has not been properly defined. The easiest solution to this is to change b.py to import a.py within g():

```
x = 1


def g():
  import a    # This will be evaluated only when g() is called
  print a.f()
```

This time when you try to import it, everything will work as you wanted it to.

```
>>> import b
>>> b.g()
1        # Printed a first time since module 'a' calls 'print f()' at the end
1        # Printed a second time, this one is our call to 'g'
```

Name clashing with library modules – One of the advantages of Python is that it comes with so many library modules. Even though this is nice, if you are not experienced or looking out for it, running into name clashes between one of your own modules and one in the library can happen. This can cause complicated issues because Python will attempt to import another library which leads to trying to import the Python standard version. When this happens the system does not know which to import, the solution to this is to be careful when choosing names.

Python 2 and Python 3 – Some people prefer to use different versions of Python, and failing to understand that can lead to issues. Look at this:

```python
import sys

def bar(i):
    if i == 1:
        raise KeyError(1)
    if i == 2:
        raise ValueError(2)

def bad():
    e = None
    try:
        bar(int(sys.argv[1]))
    except KeyError as e:
        print('key error')
    except ValueError as e:
        print('value error')
    print(e)

bad()
```

This code runs properly on Python 2:

```
$ python foo.py 1
```

key error

1

$ python foo.py 2

value error

2

If you try it on Python 3 though, this is what happened:

$ python3 foo.py 1

key error

Traceback (most recent call last):

  File "foo.py", line 19, in <module>

   bad()

  File "foo.py", line 17, in bad

   print(e)

UnboundLocalError: local variable 'e' referenced before assignment

Obviously, it doesn't work on Python 3, the reason for this is that in Python 3, the exception object can be accessed passed the scope of the except block. The best way to avoid this is to make sure there is a reference to the exception object outside the scope of the except block so it stays accessible. This is applied to the last example, making it compatible in both Python 2 and Python 3.

```
import sys

def bar(i):

    if i == 1:

        raise KeyError(1)

    if i == 2:

        raise ValueError(2)
```

```
def good():
    exception = None
    try:
        bar(int(sys.argv[1]))
    except KeyError as e:
        exception = e
        print('key error')
    except ValueError as e:
        exception = e
        print('value error')
    print(exception)
good()
```

Not using the _del_ method properly –

Let's assume you had the following in a file titled mod.py

```
import foo
class Bar(object):
        ...
    def __del__(self):
        foo.cleanup(self.myhandle)
```

Then assume you attempted to do the following from another_mod.py:

```
import mod

mybar = mod.Bar()
```

This will yield an AtrributeError exception, because when the interpreter shuts down global variables are all set to None. This means that when _del_ is used, the name foo has already been set to None. The way to fix this is to use atexit.register(), it will make it so that when your program finishes executing, the registered handlers will be kicked off before the interpreter is shut down. The solution looks like this:

```
import foo

import atexit

def cleanup(handle):

    foo.cleanup(handle)

class Bar(object):

    def __init__(self):

        ...

        atexit.register(cleanup, self.myhandle)
```

Adding this creates a reliable and clean way of using any necessary cleanup functionality of normal program termination. Of course, it will be to foo.cleanup choose what to do with the object with the name self.myhandle, so make sure it set up properly.

When you first start using your Raspberry Pi, errors are probably going to a common issue and some of them are much easier to fix than others. Sometimes, you can look at what you typed and immediately find your mistake, other times, it might feel as though you have been staring at the screen with no idea what went wrong or why. Just know, that there is a solution out there and if it is not listed in this book, with a time and effort, you will find the solution. Once you do, feel free to share it with others on forums or Q and A sites to share your new found knowledge and to further the learning community that Raspberry Pi perpetuates and encourages.

Chapter 8: Sample Project Ideas

After learning the basics of Raspberry Pi, its specification, installation and programming, it is time for you to go out and try those projects. There are so many different projects, varying drastically in difficulty. Some of them serve a very specific and useful purpose, while others are simply meant to be fun, but still educational. Regardless of the reason for the project, you will learn a lot along the way and will have a better understanding of how things work in the end.

Not all projects are created equal, some will be more difficult than others and some will require a long list of necessities. The list below leaves out any projects that involves soldering because that is not necessary in order to use the Raspberry Pi. In case you are still stuck, we have some ideas for you:

Create a Pi-Point:

There are spots in your own home where the Wi-Fi doesn't reach. Why fear when Raspberry Pi is here. Just use a Wi-Fi dongle connected to your Raspberry Pi, if it as an older model that is not wifi capable, and a MicroSD card with the software installed in it and roam around the house with a dongle in your pocket and extend you wireless signal! Not only can you extend your wi-fi connection, but you can also create a hotspot and create a guest network that is firewalled from through your home network.

To do this project, you will need:

- A Raspberry Pi
- An SD Card

First, start by downloading Raspbian from the Raspberry Pi Website. That site is: www.raspberrypi.com/downloads. Then you will install that image to your SD card.

Next, login to your Pi. The default login details are:

Username: pi

Password: raspberry

Run the command **sudo raspi-config** if you have not set up your Pi yet. After that, you'll need to install Aptitude. You do this by running **apt-get install aptitude.**

After Aptitude is running you will need to install **aptitude install rfkill zd1211-firmware hostapd hostap-utils iw dnsmasq.**

That is a very essential part to the success of this project. This command includes the installation of:

rfkill- This is the wireless utility

zd1211-firmware- This deals with zd1211 wireless hardware

hostapd- The hostap WAP daemon

hostap-utils- These are just utilities that go with hostap

iw- This is your wireless configuration utility

dnsmasq- DHCP and DNS utility

Next, you will need to add a few lines to the end of your **/etc/dhcpcd.conf file** and they are:

interface wlan0

static ip_address=192.168.1.1/24

static routers=192.168.0.1

static domain_name_servers=8.8.8.8 8.8.4.4

These tell dhcpcd statically configure the WLAN0 interface with the IP address: 192.168.1.1

Now you will need to configure your hostap. Change **/etc/hostapd/hostapd.conf** to appear this way:

interface=wlan0

driver=nl80211

ssid=test

channel=1

> TIP: hostap is very literal when it reads configuration files so be sure to have no spaces at the end of the lines.

The final step is to configure your dnsmasq to get an IP address for your PiPoint. It should look like this:

Never forward plain names (without a dot or domain part)

domain-needed

Only listen for DHCP on wlan0

interface=wlan0

create a domain if you want, comment it out otherwise

#domain=Pi-Point.co.uk

Create a dhcp range on your /24 wlan0 network with 12 hour lease time

dhcp-range=192.168.1.5,192.168.1.254,255.255.255.0,12h

Send an empty WPAD option. This may be REQUIRED to get windows 7 to behave.

#dhcp-option=252,"\n"

Change the dhcp range to whichever network IP range you are using.

- TIP: If you are having issues with a Windows 7 machine, uncomment the last line.

To make sure your PiPoint starts after a reboot create a file called **/etc/init.d/pipoint** and inside it place:

```
#!/bin/sh
# Configure Wifi Access Point.
#
### BEGIN INIT INFO
# Provides: WifiAP
# Required-Start: $remote_fs $syslog $time
# Required-Stop: $remote_fs $syslog $time
# Should-Start: $network $named slapd autofs ypbind nscd nslcd
# Should-Stop: $network $named slapd autofs ypbind nscd nslcd
# Default-Start: 2
# Default-Stop:
# Short-Description: Wifi Access Point configuration
# Description: Sets forwarding, starts hostap, enables NAT in iptables
### END INIT INFO


# turn on forwarding
echo 1 > /proc/sys/net/ipv4/ip_forward
# enable NAT
iptables -t nat -A POSTROUTING -j MASQUERADE
# start the access point
hostapd -B /etc/hostapd/hostapd.conf
```

chmod +x /etc/init.d/pipoint makes the script executable **and update-rc.d pipoint start 99 2** adds the script to the startup.

PiPoint should now reboot as a wireless internet access point.

Home Arcade Box:

Who doesn't want an arcade box at home? Even though the Raspberry Pi isn't powerful enough to support modern games it still has the ability to run the classics. Emulators are available online which can help you support outdated consoles like the Sega Genesis, SNES or even the PlayStation PC which is available on CD ROMs. Though most of us run Raspberry Pi on Raspbian Operating Systems, guys from RetroPie spent a lot of time in developing and recreating custom disk image to play some of the older titles. Road Rash anyone?

This is a pretty simple tutorial on how to achieve maximum gaming. What you will need:

- Raspberry Pi
- USB controller
- Micro SD Card- At least 4 GB
- TV
- HDMI or AV Cables
- Power Supply

- NOTE: You can find a list of all compatible accessories on the Raspberry Pi Wiki.

The first step is to download and install RetroPi on your SD card.

You will do this by visiting https://retropie.org.uk/download/ and clicking on the version of Raspberry Pi that you have. When it is done downloading you need to extract the image to your SD card. If you are using Windows, try Win32DiskImager and for Mac try RPI-SD Card Builder. Then remove the SD card and place it into your Pi.

After this you will need to boot up your Raspberry Pi. Plug your keyboard and controller in your Pi, insert the SD card and boot it up. After a few minutes, it should boot directly to the EmulationStation and this is where you configure your controller. Since it is the first time you are turning it on, you will need to follow the prompts to set up the controller. When that is done, you can use your controller to pilot through your emulators and RetroPie. Here you can also set hot keys for frequently used actions such as save and exit.

Next you will set up your Wi-Fi, scroll down to "Configure Wi-Fi" and use the action button to select it. Click on "Set Up Network", select your network, type in your passcode, and hit okay.

Next you will copy your ROMs over to your Pi. To do this you should make sure your internet connection is working properly. Then, if you are using Windows, open file manager and type in **//retropie** and if you are using a Mac open your finder, select Go> Connect to Server, type in **smb://retropie,** and connect. Now you will be able to easily remotely transfer ROM's from one device to the another! Once everything is transferred, reboot you Pi with your controller plugged in and you should be good to go!

- TIP: If you would much rather use a USB drive to store your ROM's it is very simple to do. Put them on the USB drive in a folder called "retropie" and then plug it in!

Media center:

Using Raspberry Pi for you home media center is one of the best applications of the board. You can hook up your TV through the HDMI cable for high quality screening and you can get all the media you need in your living room without having to invest in an Apple TV. Operating systems such as the RasPlex and RaspbMC have great specifications designed for you to get started on this media center. These systems can access media from remote locations or media stored in remote locations, that is, if t is connected to the Wi-Fi and helps you co-ordinate your digital data. Here is what you will need:

- Raspberry Pi
- HDMI cable
- 8 GB SD card
- USB keyboard and mouse
- Internet, Ethernet is suggested, but a good wireless connection will also work
- USB power cable
- Remote control
- USB hard drive, this is optional, it is meant for those who do not want stream movies.
- Case for the Raspberry Pi, this is also optional.
- 3.5 mm stereo audio cable, this is meant for external speakers.
- Raspmc installer, which can be found on the Raspmc website, it will need to be on the SD card.

First, before anything is hooked up to the television, you will need to download Raspmc and put it on the SD card. The installer is free from the website, and should download easily.

Once the software is on the card, you can now hook the Raspberry Pi to the television. This should be easy since you just plug in all the cables in their designated spots. Make sure the power supply is also plugged into the wall. Once it is plugged in, it will begin the boot up process from the SD card.

This is the boring part since you don't need to do anything during the next step except wait. It will probably take about 15 to 25 minutes for it to start, but once it does, it will be ready for you to make adjustments, once it is finished it will say XMBC, which is the software you are actually running on your media center.

Change the settings to what suits your needs, such as the resolution. One of the common issues people run is that the image is stretched beyond on their screen, this can be easily fixed using the overscan wizard. It can be found in Settings > System > Video Output > Video Calibration, then all you need to do is change the settings to make it fit your screen.

XMBC needs separate folders for movies and television shows, and then just drag them into the corresponding folder on your USB hard drive. Make sure they have the appropriate name format such as Tron.2010.mkv, some people also include the resolution in the name so they can see if it is necessary to change the settings before the movie begins. This can save time, but if all your videos are the same resolution, it is not necessary.

This is a basic set up for beginners and although it is efficient and convenient, it should be known that there are some things it is not capable of doing such as playing MPEG – 2 videos or streaming from the internet, like Netflix.

Wireless Control of your stereo:

Though there are many advancements happening in the audio technology that has helped you carry your tunes with you wherever you go, some of us like to listen to our beats in a loud, surround sound fashion. RuneAudio disk image will help you achieve your goal. By connecting it to your Raspberry Pi, you can remotely control all the appliances in your home audio setup. Irrespective of it being stored locally on one of your devices or a remote device, you can search, organize and play tracks through your browser or your smartphone while connected to the internet. For this. You will need:

- USB power supply, there are many different options, but one as close to 5V DC is best.
- 8 GB SD card

- Card reader, if your computer does not have one already.
- Hard drive or jump drive
- Internet connection

First you will need to download and extract the RuneAudio software and put it on your SD card. When it has finished writing to the card, safely remove it from your computer and put it in the Raspberry Pi.

Next you will need to prepare the Raspberry Pi, this means plugging everything in where it needs to go and make sure to include the PSU as well, then turn it on.

Rune will now boot and while doing so, it will acquire an IP address. You can connect to Rune in three ways; looking up the IP address, going to the website, and for Windows users, a new icon will pop up on their computer.

Rune will automatically scan your music library and convert it to an internet database, but in order for this to happen, Rune needs to know where your music is. The easiest way to do this is to just use a USB hard drive since it will automatically be detected and scanned. After waiting a few minutes for it to scan and generate your library, you are ready to use Rune. The default settings are meant to be kept, because it is easy to accidentally mess something up, this might lead to having to start all over again. So only tweak the settings if you are confident you understand exactly what you are doing.

Make your own phone:

With a similar phones popping in every corner, we are lacking of choice between iPhone, android and a Windows phone. Then it time to make you own PiPhone! Thanks to Raspberry Pi's versatility, it is able to make host of connections and turning it into your new phone is not going to take too much effort. All you need to buy is a battery pack, as GSM module, a compatible touch screen and you have all the hardware requirements to create your next new phone. You can run your phone on the software already available in the market or hook up with some tutorials online to connect to all Apple store, Google play and the Microsoft Apps. Or simply download the apk file and run it with your smartphone. Although, this is not considered a difficult project, it does require many different items and some of them can be expensive, just keep that in mind when you begin. Here is what you will need:

- Duct tape
- Cables
- Zip ties
- Sim card
- 5 VC DC-DC converter
- Foam board, cut to the size of the Raspberry Pi
- Headphones
- Microphone
- Electrical switch
- Velcro squares
- Touch screen
- GSM/GPRS module with antenna and audio outlets
- Battery Pack
- Raspberry Pi running Python

First, you will need to put everything on the Raspberry Pi, as mentioned above, Python will be used as well as Piphone software which is available for free online and Wirehunt, also a free download. So, the first step is to put all of this on the Raspberry Pi. Once, all of this is on the device, connect it to the touchscreen.

Now you will need power, so use the cables and connect the battery to the switch, then connect the switch to the GSM module. Next, you will need to connect the GSM header to the DC-DC converter. Now, you will need to link this to the Raspberry Pi using another cable. The Raspberry Pi will also need to be connected via cables from the transmit pins to the GSM module as well, these are also known as the

Rx and Tx ports. Once this has been completed, simply insert the sim card.

Now you will need to assemble the parts, begin by placing the Raspberry Pi on the foam board. Use the Velcro squares and the duct tape to attach the GSM module, converter, and the switch on the other side of the foam. Put the battery between the screen and the Raspberry Pi, but make sure not to leave it turned on for all of this because it can get too hot.

Now, everything is ready to be used. Just turn it on and dial a number you wish to call. Remember, this is just a basic phone. What you choose to do with it from here is up to you, but this gave you a great starting foundation. Some people choose to use software that allows them to run Android or Apple apps. There are many different possibilities.

Dive into the Future with a smart mirror:

Have you ever watched a sci-fi movie and gawked over the gadgets just hoping that technology would catch up to the movies? With Raspberry Pi, you can turn any ordinary two-way mirror into a smart mirror. This mirror can display the weather, the time, and the news amongst other things. To start this project, you will need a few major things such as a tablet running Android, a cellular device running Android, and a 42-inch television with an HDMI port. Though this project is a bit time consuming, it is certainly an ice-breaker for any awkward situations you may be in!

This tutorial requires some carpentry, so you may need to get your hands dirty! What you will need:

- A monitor with an HDMI port, with the HDMI port near the middle
- A double-sided mirror
- Some 2x4's for the case
- Thin wood or corkboard

- A Raspberry Pi and its accessories i.e. power supply, HDMI, etc.
- Saw, sandpaper, and screwdrivers
- Screws

The first thing you will need to do is remove the casing from the monitor, make sure to be very careful with the wiring as it is very delicate.

Now, to build the case, remember the carpentry previously mentioned? We are about to put it to use. Depending on the size of monitor that you have chosen you will use your saw to cut the 2x4's so that your monitor fits very snuggly.

> TIP: Make sure to drill holes in the frame, not only for your Pi to breathe but also to be able to run the power supply!

Next, you will build the frame. This is the hardest part by far. The easiest thing I can say to do is either buy liquid nails and a 90-degree angle clamp, they are usually around $20 and after you cut the wood and sand it down to fit on the case.

Double-sided mirrors are easy to cut so fitting the mirror to the case and frame should be very easy with the right tools.

> TIP: If you are going to stain the frame and case, be sure to do so before gluing the mirror in.

Now, you need to attach the Raspberry Pi to your monitor. It is much easier if there is only one cord coming from the bottom of the case, so a power splitter, they are inexpensive and are much easier than splicing wires.

Connect your Pi to your monitor and set the monitor softly into the case against the frame. It should all fit very well together if you made sure to measure properly. Now, power up your Raspberry Pi, connect your Pi to your router using an Ethernet cable, and install Raspian. After that is installed, it is time to install Chromium. Depending on the version of Pi you have, the command lines can vary but this one seems to work for most to install Chromium.

wget http://ftp.us.debian.org/debian/pool/main/libg/libgcrypt11/libgcrypt11_1.5.0-5+deb7u3_armhf.deb

wget http://launchpadlibrarian.net/218525709/chromium-browser_45.0.2454.85-0ubuntu0.14.04.1.1097_armhf.deb

wget http://launchpadlibrarian.net/218525711/chromium-codecs-ffmpeg-extra_45.0.2454.85-0ubuntu0.14.04.1.1097_armhf.deb

sudo dpkg -i libgcrypt11_1.5.0-5+deb7u3_armhf.deb

sudodpkg-ichromium-codecs-ffmpeg-extra_45.0.2454.85 0ubuntu0.14.04.1.1097_armhf.deb

sudo dpkg -i chromium-browser_45.0.2454.85-0ubuntu0.14.04.1.1097_armhf.deb

With Chromium installed you may now move on to configuring it to open on startup in full screen mode. You do this by opening the auto start settings.

sudo nano /etc/xdg/lxsession/LXDE-pi/autostart

Now disable the screen saver by adding a # right before:

@xscreensaver -no-splash

Now add these lines:

@xset s off @xset -dpms @xset s noblank /usr/bin/chromium --noerrdialogs --kiosk --incognito "http://localhost"

Save and exit to confirm that you want the screensaver disabled, the power management settings disabled, and Chromium opening in kiosk mode on localhost when you start up.

Next, you need to connect to your internet. Do this by editing your wpa_supplicant file.

sudo nano /etc/network/interfaces

Then edit the network settings:

network={ ssid="Network name here" psk="password" }

Change the network name to your network and the password to your password to access your internet.

Restart your Wi-Fi connection using the command:

ifdown wlano ifup wlano

Once your device is assigned an IP address you may now disconnect your Ethernet cable and attach the backing to the case. The backing can be a thin piece of wood attached to the case via screws in the case or you can use corkboard and glue it to the case. The thin piece of wood is much more durable.

You will need a web server to host a webpage and a php to run Lumen. You can do this by entering:

sudo apt-get update sudo apt-get install nginx php5-fpm php5-cli php5-mcrypt git

This may take a while and once it is done you will need to configure nginx to know where your MirrorMirror site is located. Do this by entering the following mirror.config:

sudo nano /etc/nginx/sites-available/mirror.conf

Initiate the configuration by running:

sudo ln -s /etc/nginx/sites-available/mirror.conf /etc/nginx/sites-enabled/mirror.conf sudo service nginx reload

Now onto the final step!

Make a folder called "projects" in your /home/pi and move it to:

mkdir /home/pi/projects cd /home/pi/projects

Now clone the mirror app with:

git clone https://github.com/ctrlaltdylan/MirrorMirror.git

Install Composer which will Lumen's dependencies with:

curl -sS https://getcomposer.org/installer | sudo php -- --install-dir=/usr/local/bin --filename=composer

Now use Composer to get MirrorMirror running with:

cd MirrorMirror composer install

Nginx needs to have the ability to read and write files into storage to work properly, you can do this by using the command:

sudo chmod -R 777 storage

Your new mirror should be ready to go!

Get rid of those pesky internet ads by building a PiHole:

You're browsing away catching up on the news when suddenly, it happens. You begin to get pop-up after pop-up, the website you are on has so many ads that you can barely read the content without bursting a blood vessel in frustration. No need to fret, PiHole is here to help! By changing a few settings on your router and changing a few lines on your Pi, you can build an endless black hole that sucks in ads from over 155,000 domains. No more clicking the exit button until your fingers hurt!

Remember though, that many websites operate with the money generated with ads, so if everyone did this, websites would not be able to operate. So many people still allow for popups, but only from some websites, generally the ones they use the most. Again, this is up to you, but keep it in mind when you are setting up our PiHole. This is what you will need:

- Internet connection, either wireless or through an Ethernet cord.
- Keyboard for installation
- Raspberry Pi

- Power supply

You will need both Raspbian and Diet Pi to be installed on your SD card for installation, which are both found easily online with a simple search. For this project, we will assume you will be working with a Windows computer, so first you are going to download the PiHole software and unzip the contents. Put this on the SD card and wait until it finishes writing before safely removing it and putting into your Raspberry Pi.

Next, you will connect both the keyboard, power supply, and Ethernet cable to the Raspberry Pi and wait for it to boot. The Raspberry Pi will probably restart boot many times before it finally finishes to a startup screen, this is perfectly normal, so don't be worried and just let it finish.

When you get to the startup screen, login with the username; root, and the password: dietpi. Doing this will allow the Raspberry Pi to look for and install any necessary updates, so let it so if necessary. Once it is finished, you will need to reboot and login again.

Once all of this is finished you will end up at the DietPi setup screen where you will need to set up a static IP address. This is crucial because it means your Raspberry Pi will be available for many different devices. This is how you do this:

- Choose Okay on the first startup screen.
- Click on Change Wired Network Settings.
- Click on Change Mode and then hit enter to change it to static.
- Choose copy current address to static, and make sure you write it down because you will using it later.
- Click on apply to save the changes and then restart the network.

Once you have finished these steps, click on Exit which will restart the Raspberry Pi one more time.

Now you will need to install the PiHole software, which might take around half an hour or more. Once that has finally finished installing, your system will shut down and restart again, but this time it will be running the new software.

After all of that has finished, all that is left is to route traffic through it because it is this that allows for ad blocking. For this to work properly, you must change your devices' DNS settings, doing this means that all devices will ping through the Raspberry Pi, but only if they are all on the same network. This is how to do so:

Right click on the Start button and click on Network Connections.

Choose your own Wifi or Ethernet network.

Click on Internet Protocol Version 4.

Choose Use the following DNS server addresses.

Where it says the Preferred DNS server, type in your Raspberry Pi's static IP address.

When you are using your PiHole, if you find you do need popups for certain sites to operate properly, you can whitelist certain sites to allow them through on all devices. This is how you do this:

On the Raspberry Pi's command line enter cd **/etc/pihole/** and type in **nano whitelist.txt** which will open a new text file.

Enter the webite url's for any sites you wish to allow popups from, make sure to hit enter between them.

Then hit control and x, this will both save and exit.

Lastly, restart your Raspberry Pi and once it has rebooted the changes you made will have already taken effect.

There are many different updates that involve whitelisting, so by the time you need it, looking for newer, easier techniques might be in your best interest.

Display all your photos with the Pi powered photo frame:

We have seen the interactive photo frames that you can buy from various locations and they are pretty cool, but he PiFrame makes it a bit more interactive!

What you will need:

- A Raspberry Pi
- A micro SD card—Preferably over 8 GB
- External Hard Drive or USB Drive
- Touch Screen with an HDMI port, you can buy the official Pi touchscreen from their website or from other various online sellers.

Before starting, make sure to set up your Wi-Fi connection, you can find excellent tutorials online to teach you how to do so!

We will first start out with the software side of things. The screen will go blank after 10 minutes, we want to disable that. To do that, enter:

sudo nano /etc/lightdm/lightdm.conf

This will open the lightdm.conf file which controls the sleep settings of the pie. Once you are in the folder enter the following anywhere beneath the line that reads [seatdefaults]:

xserver-command=X -s 0 —dpms

To save and exit hit Control+x and the y

Now reboot using:

sudo reboot

The Pi will no longer go black after 10 minutes.

Now we will set up the slideshow using the FEH package, it is simple and very user friendly, especially for a beginner.

sudo apt-get install feh

You will want to test to make sure that it has worked, to do so, type the following command but change /media/NASHDD1/test with the directory that contains your media:

DISPLAY=:0.0   XAUTHORITY=/home/pi/.Xauthority /usr/bin/feh --quiet --preload --randomize --full-screen -- reload 60 -Y --slideshow-delay 15.0 /media/NASHDD1/test

Now you can use short tags to make the command much shorter, you do this by typing in the following command but change /media/NASHDD1/test with the directory that contains your media:

DISPLAY=:0.0   XAUTHORITY=/home/pi/.Xauthority /usr/bin/feh   -q   -p   -Z   -F   -R   60   -Y   -D   15.0 /media/NASHDD1/test

> **TIP:** You will see that this command locks up the command line bar, to fix this issue simply add the '&' symbol after the command that the process will start in the background.

Now you will need to save this script file do so by entering:

sudo nano /home/pi/start-picture-frame.sh

After you have access to this file enter the following command in the folder. Again, change /media/NASHDD1/test with the directory that contains your media:

DISPLAY=:0.0   XAUTHORITY=/home/pi/.Xauthority /usr/bin/feh   -q   -p   -Z   -F   -R   60   -Y   -D   15.0 /media/NASHDD1/test

Now that you have entered that into the folder you may test it by running:

bash /home/pi/start-picture-frame.sh

If everything works well, it is time to move on to have it start when you boot your Pi up. To do so enter the command to open your rc.local file:

sudo nano /etc/rc.local

Before the 'exit 0' line, add the following:

bash /home/start-picture-frame.sh &

Now save, exit, and reboot and you should have your very own interactive photo frame!

Protect your belongings with a PiCam:

Security cameras can be a bit pricey with some being over $100 for one single camera! That can get to be too much, but you don't have to break your wallet to protect yourself and the things that you love. Build a PiCam!

What you will need:

- Raspberry Pi 3
- Raspberry Pi camera, which you can buy from their website
- A power supply
- A micro SD card

The first thing you will need to do is to physically install the Raspberry Pi camera. You do this by locating the ribbon slot directly behind the Ethernet port and gently lifting the clasps that are pushed down. The port is now open and you can insert the ribbon that is attached to the camera with the metal leads pointing away from the Ethernet port. Now gently close the clasps and we will move on to the software!

Download MotionPie SD Card Image from from the MotionPie website. Next you will need to download SD Formatter 4.0 from the SD Card Association.

Insert your SD card into your SD card reader and use the SD Formatter to your micro SD.

Now, download Win32DiskImager this will help you install MotionPie. First unzip the file so as to install it to your Pi safely. Open Win32 and select the MotionPie zip file and the SD card that you would like it to be written on, then hit write. Once that is done, you can eject and remove your SD safely.

Now insert your SD card into your Pi, connect your Ethernet cord, connect the power supply, and boot up your Raspberry Pi.

When you are fully booted, you will need to figure out your IP address for your Pi. For Windows, go to Network on the right hand side of the file explorer and you should see the name of the computer, for instance DS-L345DCF.

Now, go to your browser and type in the following, replacing the example with your device.

http://MP-E28D9CE5

The MotionPie interface should now be up and login. Click the key at the top and type in the user name and password the default user name and password is:

Username: admin

Password:--This is left blank---

This is where you can change all of the settings for your camera.

You now have a working security camera!

Many people find that they just wanted to complete their project and then move onto something else more difficult or challenging. That is the beauty of the Raspberry Pi, you can simply take it apart and start all over. Nothing is permanent, not even the case it is held in. There are so many possibilities and the more comfortable and confident you become, more complex projects will likely follow. It is not necessary to own a soldering gun to create intricate and functional projects, however, that is a possibility if you so choose. Others take as much joy in designing the cases their Raspberry Pi will be encased in just as much as the project themselves. For instance, you can make and paint a frame for your interactive mirror that matches the décor in your home, or you could come up with an elaborate set up for your vintage gaming console that looks like it came out of a different decade. With the Raspberry Pi, you have the option and the power to do almost anything you would like with it.

Tips and Tricks!

I'm sure you're very excited to start exploring your new Raspberry Pi, so here are some things to get you started in the right direction. This section will teach you about what you need to get your Pi up and running and easy commands that will help you along the way. Again, some of you might be completely new to this, so you are in essence learning how to use the words you already know in completely new ways, so it might take some time before it feels as though it comes naturally to you. However, with some patience and determination you will be completing projects and maybe even inventing your own in no time at all.

So, what do you need to get started with your Pi? To keep the price low, the manufacturers had to make some important decisions which meant excluding many of the things that would come with a new computer in the box.

Things you will absolutely need to get started:

A power supply: The Raspberry Pi 3 is powered with a +5.1V micro USB supply. So, buying a 2.5-amp power supply will be enough to power your new Pi. You can buy this directly from the Raspberry Pi website or through a reputable dealer.

A monitor: This is obviously up to the user with regards to size and brand. It is however, recommended that you purchase a monitor that has an HDMI port because the Raspberry Pi 3 connects more fluidly with HDMI.

USB keyboard: This is also up to the user, there are no recommendations, whatever you are comfortable with.

A mouse: A USB powered mouse.

SD memory card: It is recommended to get at least 4 GB but, the more memory in the SD card the more you will be able to store.

Ethernet cable: This is to connect your Pi to your router.

These are some essential commands to get you started, these are basic commands that are necessary to learn. These will help you with the general operation of the software and the Raspberry Pi itself. Most people find that it doesn't take very long for them to memorize these commands which makes their work much easier and a lot more fluid. If you find yourself looking them up, don't fret, like with any language, it will be easier with repetition.

General commands:

apt-get update: This will update your version of Raspian

apt-get upgrade: This upgrades the software in your Pi

clear: This tells the terminal screen to clear all previous commands

date: This prints the current date

poweroff: Shuts down power immediately

raspi-config: Opens the configuration settings menu

reboot: Reboots the system immediately

shutdown -h now: Shuts down the Pi immediately

shutdown -h 01:22: Shuts down the system at 1:22 A.M. You can change this to any time you would like it to shut down automatically.

Networking and Internet Commands:

ifconfig: This checks the status of the wireless internet you are using

iwlist wlan0 scan: Prints a list of the available wireless internet

ping: This tests the connectivity between two things, even website. For example:

ping www.google.com

System Information Commands:

cat /proc/meminfo: This displays information about your memory

cat /proc/partitions: This shows the size and the number of partitions on your SD card or any other memory device

cat /proc/version: This shows what version of Raspberry Pi you are using

df -h: This shows information about the disk space you have available

df /: This shows how much disk space you have available

free: Shows the amount free memory available

hostname -I: This displays the IP address for your Pi

lsusb: Gives a list of the hardware attached via USB

vcgencmd measure_temp: Displays the temperature of your CPU

Now that you have the essentials to physically start your Pi and you have some basic commands, it is up to you to decide what you want to do next. There are so many projects that all of them could not even begin to be listed here. No matter how big or small, there is something for you to do with your Pi!

This is a solid foundation that you have created that will allow you to explore a part of our world that you might not have had a good understanding of yesterday. Remember, the Raspberry Pi is meant for teaching so there is a wealth of information available online about common errors and mistakes. If you run into an issue, chances are, you will not be the first person to have that problem. So, a simple internet search might give you the solution you have been looking for. There are several forums to find exactly what you are looking for, even if it is as small as not being able to connect a certain keyboard. Instead of getting frustrated and giving up, devote some time to finding the answer and move forward. It will be worth it!

Conclusion

Learning about computational concepts and devices help us grow and move forward in the technological race that humanity is running in. Though mathematics and algorithms are seen as boring and dry subjects, it becomes interesting once you are able to comprehend and apply it in a real world scenario. Raspberry Pi believes in this dream of promoting math, science, engineering and technology to everyone and keep pace with the ever changing world. Come to think of it, these concepts and projects that can be derived from the Raspberry Pi makes me more interested and curious about the places that we can use in our day to day life.

I hope you got a great insight to the world of Raspberry Pi, its construction, components, working, programming and execution. Raspberry Pi seems to look like a very elementary version of a computer, so basic, and yet the outcomes of the device are explosive. Its unique capability to fit itself in any place inconspicuously is ironically what makes it stand out in the industry. Besides the fact that it is educational and useful, its low prices attract many students across borders to buy and play around with it.

Thank you for choosing to purchase this book. I hope this book has inspired you to go online and purchase a Raspberry Pi board and experiment with it. This book is aimed at motivating people to get you more interested and involved in inventing new technology that makes our lives easier. Who knows these boards and concept might help your brain concoct the next best technology or application that would revolutionize the world!